M000034730

Do As I Say,

Not As I Did

Most Perigee Books are available at special quantity discounts for bulk purchases for sales promotions, premiums, fund-raising or educational use. Special books, or book excerpts, can also be created to fit specific needs.

For details, write: Special Markets, The Berkley Publishing Group, 200 Madison Avenue, New York, New York 10016.

Do As I Say,

Not As I Did

Perfect Advice from an Imperfect Mother

Wendy Reid Crisp

A Perigee Book

A Perigee Book
Published by The Berkley Publishing Group
200 Madison Avenue
New York, NY 10016

Copyright ©1997 by Wendy Reid Crisp

All rights reserved. This book, or parts thereof, may not be
reproduced in any form without permission.

First edition: May 1997
ISBN: 0-399-52334-0

Published simultaneously in Canada.

The Putnam Berkley World Wide Web site address is
http://www.berkley.com

Printed in the United States of America

10 9 8 7 6 5 4 3 2 1

For Nicole, Caroline, and Lynne:
my daughter, my stepdaughter,
and my daughter-in-law;
for Maxine, my own imperfect mother;
and for Zelma, who is perfect.
May our tribe increase.

Thank you

Maximilian Crisp, Adele Crawford, Dan Siger, Pat Mauney, Joan Saxe, David Jackson, Carolyn Wheatley, Steve Schilling, Sue Laris-Eastin, Linda Russ, Suzanne Bober, Carla Glasser, Jill Mason, Laine Latimer, Jody Fleury, Dee Johnson, Bob Wood, Giuliana Halasz, Ann Landi, Pat McCormick, Tonya Detlefsen, and, especially, Bill Zavin.

Introduction

Many years ago, before ATMs and VCRs and Cuisinarts, so long ago that Gloria Steinem was still a Playboy bunny and single women were turned down for Sears credit cards (why would an old maid want a lawn mower?)—that many years ago, in the city of Pasadena, California, there lived an old woman, a dowager over fifty, who practiced the magic of psychology. One day, a young princess went to see her. The princess was unhappy, strangely, vaguely unhappy, and she didn't know why.

"Is it your marriage?" the old woman asked.

"Oh, no, no, no!" cried the princess. "That is not the answer. My marriage is perfect."

Ten times the princess went to the old woman, and ten times she gave the same response. On the eleventh visit, the old woman said, "Tell me the many ways your marriage is perfect, so I may learn your secrets and use them to help others."

The princess said nothing. Then the tears

began to fall. "It is my marriage; it's lonely and sad. My husband is a prince, but . . . "

The old woman handed the princess a Kleenex and said softly, "Why don't you get a divorce? You have no children, you have no property, the two of you share nothing but a cat."

The princess gasped in horror. "I could never, ever, ever get a divorce!" she said.

"Why not?" asked the old woman.

Pale and shaking, the princess replied, "Because I can't face starting all over."

With that, the old woman—who was also a big woman—leaned dangerously backward in her chair and laughed a big woman's laugh.

"Honey," she said, because this was in the days before the New Language, "Honey, at twenty-five, you haven't even started for the first time."

And then the old woman told the princess that life is nothing if not a series of endings and beginnings, and that one must be ready to start over and over again throughout the years, and that if one morning a person wakes up and truly can't face starting over one more time, she shouldn't bother to get out of bed. "If you can't start over," the old woman counseled, "it *is* over."

"My family will be devastated," the princess said. "If I get a divorce, it will ruin their lives."

The old woman nodded and gave the

princess a second piece of advice, like the first, more valuable than a gold coin.

"What other people think doesn't matter," she said, "because other people don't think about you that much."

In this story, as in all fairy tales, everything happens in threes. The princess had one last question.

"Everyone will ask me why I'm getting a divorce. What do I tell them?" The old woman brought out her third piece of advice.

"All your life people will always ask you questions you don't want to answer," she said. "When they do, look very grave, and say, 'It just didn't work out.' And then stop talking. If anyone ever pushes you for more information—and almost no one ever will—you say, "*Well*, it just didn't work out."

It is perhaps not fair to present those three pieces of wisdom as the only advice I received in my early adulthood. I do recall asking my parents if I, newly divorced, should buy the house I was renting. "Absolutely not," I was told. "Someday, you may remarry and the man you may meet may not want to live there." Fortunately for my future economic stability, I already understood the word "equity."

Now, I want my daughter—and my step-daughter and my daughter-in-law—to profit from the lessons I learned. I want their lives to be rich, rewarding, and full of delights. I want to put my arms around them and protect them from loneliness and fear and things that go bump—even in the daytime, when they're least expecting it.

But they won't let me. So I had to write this book.

Wendy Reid Crisp
Portland, Oregon
January 1997

Do As I Say,

Not As I Did

Reconsider piercing your face.

I didn't say too much when your brother had a
butterfly the size of a number ten envelope
tattooed on his left shoulder while I was in
Minneapolis giving a speech on "How to
Manage Your Life." But I'm home more often
now, and my guilt level has subsided. My great-
grandmother's ruby solitaire as a nose stud is an
interesting fashion update; still, I'd suggest you
hold off on permanent disfiguration until you're
absolutely certain you will never need gainful
employment.

When a boss asks you for your "honest opinion," don't give it.

What is being requested ("What do you think? I should've fired him months ago, right?") is a *supportive* response ("Absolutely. No question. You were brilliant."), not an *independent* opinion.

This is not the time to think, "Wow! At last, my intelligence and perspective are appreciated—guess I'll open the floodgates of advice." Instead, unveil the graciousness with which you responded to the roommate who was clearly enchanted with her sequined mini

wedding dress rather than the brutal objectivity
you displayed when presented with my square-
dancing skirt.

Master the mundane.

Even college graduates used to start out as receptionists and switchboard operators—like Ernestine in the reruns of *Laugh-In*. It was assumed that knowledge of the English renaissance and constitutional law would be augmented with the lore of taking phone messages, making coffee, and resetting the postage meter. Thus, power bases were built: while filing, we reviewed the company's past correspondence; we read the mail we were told to open and sort; we followed the trail of memos and deposits. Within weeks, we were the best-informed employees in the company. This is an immediate political advantage; plus, if you don't learn a profession from the ground

 up, you can forget becoming an entrepreneur. The first day you walk into your own business,

you will discover that when you put letters in your "out" basket, you have to run around to the front of the desk and mail them yourself.

Choose embarrassment over death.

An editorial assistant rushed in late to a meeting gasping, "Two weird guys followed me for blocks. I almost called the police."

"Why didn't you?" I asked.

"If I'd been wrong," she said, "I would have just died."

"And if you'd been right?"

In the middle of the night in an abandoned building some women will enter a freight elevator occupied by a deranged stranger carrying an assault rifle because they're worried about hurting his feelings.

Please don't be that nice.

Four reasons to stop the wedding.

1. I have five years in this relationship—a
    quarter of my life. I'll marry him to save the
    investment.

2. I'm not head-over-heels, but I respect him.
    This must be what they mean by "mature"
    love.

3. His mother/father/sister/grandparents are
    the family I never had.

4. Great sex! Everything else will work out.

Establish credit when you don't need it.

My generation was reared by parents who grew
up in the Great Depression and who believed
that credit was debt and debt was the work of
the devil: Buying a refrigerator *on time?* Better
you should be a topless dancer. *Car payments?*
You can't ride the bus until you've saved up?
(My parents paid *cash* for their houses—
ensuring them a rank in heaven's highest circles
and a smile from the IRS: no mortgage interest
deductions for them, no sir.) My generation,
consequently, has a dysfunctional relationship
with money that has spawned three shelves'

worth of self-help books at Barnes & Noble. Save yourself years of therapy and savor the fruits of your labors: it's a misquote that money is the root of all evil (the Bible says the *love* of money is the root of all evil, and whoever wrote that line had never run into a bottle of Chivas and a redhead in St. Louis, but that's another story).

Learn how to buy money.

Loan officers, given the choice, prefer applicants
who wear ski masks to those whose hands shake
when filling out their credit history. Banks are
not in the emergency aid business—if red ink
begins to flow from your checkbook, you can't
dial 911 and request that an armored car
manned with parafinanciers rush to your
address—banks are in the business of selling
cash. "Interest" is the price tag dangling from the
money that's for sale. It's that simple. And here's
what else is simple: banks like to sell money to
people they know—or, at least, people whom

their associates know ("credit references"). Fortunately, making friends with a bank is much easier than rushing a sorority or trying out for cheerleader or applying for mascara editor at *Elle.* Open a savings account and make a deposit for, say, $500. Wait about ten days (think of it as "simmering"). Then, go into the same bank, sit down at one of those tidy walnut desks and wait for a pleasant-faced person to acknowledge your presence (you aren't wearing jeans, of course, or your life-sized fruit bat earrings). Ask to borrow $500 for a vacation to a place from which the bank can reasonably expect you will return (postpone the trek to Kabul). When you have the check in hand, take it to another bank and use it to open a second savings account. Once a month, withdraw from the second account the exact amount necessary to pay off the loan—and pay it off as the contract states, not earlier or in misshapen lumps of cash—until the debt is cleared. Voila! You have credit. As soon as you can, borrow again and repeat the process, gradually building up the amount of money the banks are comfortable selling to you. The day will come when you can walk in and ask for a quarter of a million bucks to buy a lot on the lake, and the loan officer will say, "You bet. And hey, terrific earrings! Are those bats?"

A good man is not hard to find if you know what you're looking for.

He knows all the words to "The Star-Spangled Banner" and he stands up, removes his baseball cap, and sings as loudly as he will later shout when the ref calls Jordan's fourth technical.

What is revealed here? Reverence for country and tradition, a sense of propriety, courtesy and—particularly as he strains for "the rockets' red glare"—guts.

Abandon hope of getting enough rest.

The *Wall Street Journal* once published the results of a survey that claimed that women work three and a half hours more a day than men do. I'll do the math for you: that's twenty-four and a half hours a week—a whole 'nuther day—that we work more than they do.

 This is no surprise to those of us who know our Scriptures. The last thing God created was woman. And then he rested. *He rested.* That's how I know—discussions with feminist theologians notwithstanding—that God

is not a woman. If he were a woman, he would
have *meant* to rest, but he would have kept
jumping up to arrange another flower, tweak
the colors on one more bird. And since we're on
the subject of Eden—don't buy any of that
woman-as-evil-temptress stuff. If Adam had
been even slightly conversational, Eve wouldn't
have had to visit with a snake.

Network with unimportant people.

In the recession of 1981 (the year you wanted
to go to the camp where you would have been
given your own horse, but you had to go to the
Y day camp instead), Diane, an acquaintance,
was canned from her corporate public relations
job. Skilled in the practice of networking, she
went through her Rolodex and watched as her
prized connections vaporized. Finally, her
savings running out, she parted with $35 and
signed up for a "networking" dinner sponsored
by a women's business club. She arrived early
and sat at a round table next to another woman

in a fraying suit carrying, as she was, a portfolio. Introducing herself, Diane quickly learned, to her dismay, that the other woman, too, was also looking for work; the two commiserated. Eventually, a third woman joined the table. Ms. Right! The new guest was second-in-command of a major international communications firm, a woman who knew Diane's former clients and recognized her successful campaigns. Diane turned on the charm. Within a week, she had an interview, and then a second and a third. Three weeks after the networking dinner, she had a new job—with increased responsibilities, wider potential for creativity, and more benefits

than her former, mourned position. The lead
had come from the jobless woman in the old
suit. Diane never heard from Ms. Right.

There are no unimportant people—or,
perhaps there are, but there's no way of
recognizing them.

If you love him, lie.

Popular psychology would have us believe that the foundation of a powerful relationship is absolute truthfulness. If you're the one who's been unfaithful, however, restrain yourself. Total honesty can be a cop-out for seeking absolution. If you must confess, get yourself down to Our Lady of Martyrs, even though you're not Catholic. You can say that it's been so long since your last confession, you can't recall the ritual. The priest will appreciate the business.

Net worth does not equal self-worth.

Easy to say—that $8.20 is an acceptable
checking account balance—and furthermore, it's
safe: if that amount is displayed on an automatic
teller machine in full view of the line behind
you, you have almost no chance of being
mugged. Hard to live, though—especially when
a friend wants to meet you for lunch and you're
not sure if she means to pay—and if she doesn't
and you can't tell her, it will set you back at
least $20, and you won't have that much until
Friday.

"You are what you earn" was the motto of the '80s. Be grateful that decade has been discredited.

Fight the compulsion to be perfect.

People who hold fast to "Anything worth doing is worth doing well" dare to try something new, oh, once every ten years or so. They refuse to play the guitar in public because they know a mere six tunes; they are positive they aren't qualified for the opening in the marketing department with a B.S. in biology. Alas, when the action comes down, Little Miss Perfecto is left alone. No one wants to hang out—even temporarily—with a person who does everything well: after four strummed guitar solos, the group will move on to some amazing gossip; the person who gets the marketing job will be a bassoonist who is 20 credits short of a psych degree.

Leaders must be imperfect. Watch the dynamic in a casual group sing: if a contralto bursts into "Moon River" with a pitch worthy of the Metropolitan Opera, the room grows respectfully hushed. Let loose off-key and forget half the lyrics and miraculously, the hills are alive with the sound of something similar to music.

The truth is, anything worth doing is worth doing half-assed.

Avoid married men—and single men with an untanned circle around the third finger on their left hand.

I doubt you'll enjoy romantic red-lining: being restricted to certain restaurants in distant neighborhoods, calling him only on his office line, and spending weekends and holidays with gay friends who send you home early and hit their own parties. On the other hand, this may be your one great love, he may indeed leave the woman he accidentally married while in his Father-Knows-Best phase, and the two of you may pass the rest of your lives enthralled that you found each other. This does happen, so what's with the self-righteous sermonizing? Well, here's a formula to keep you out of a remake of *Back Street:* Ignore his desperate rationales ("I love you, but I can't leave as long as her second cousin has rheumatoid arthritis") and give him a couple of months to remove his bowling trophies and his *Civil War* tapes from her attic and himself from her boudoir (I know, I know, he sleeps in the tool shed). In the meantime, take up tap dancing and backpack through Bolivia: you're going to need new sources of self-esteem.

There are no big breaks.

We make our own breaks, not by beating
relentlessly on what we think is the door to
fame and fortune, but by polishing the tiny
scraps that scatter our way.

    A few years ago in the *New York Times*,
there was a letter from a young woman. She had
been, she said, riding downtown on the subway,
sitting, staring at the floor, not making eye
contact with the other riders, in the appropriate
and expected manner of Manhattanites
temporarily coexisting in the bowels of the
transit system. Suddenly, a lone green grape

rolled down the center of the car. She looked up slowly and caught the smile of the person seated across the aisle; she smiled. Others began to smile, to watch the grape, and to look around for the origin: a damp and broken bag; a rider picking at a cluster, carelessly scattering loosies—there was no explanation. The grape rolled along to the end of the car, out the door, and onto the tracks. The riders shared a final communal sigh, and then eyes dropped, isolation was resumed. End of letter; a New York moment.

Three weeks later, the *Times* published a follow-up. The letter writer, it transpired, was an aspiring actress—one of what? twenty thousand in New York? After her story was published, she went on an audition for a soap opera. She read, and the casting director said, "What else have you done?"

She said, "Community theater upstate, summer stock. . . . " He said, "No. Your name is familiar. I think I've seen it in print." "I had a letter in the *Times*." "Are you the woman with the grape?" She nodded, and he went on, "That eye for detail, that understanding of human behavior is the mark of a fine actress." She got the job.

There are no big breaks. There are only rolling grapes. Some people see them, and some people don't.

Test that yellow paint.

This was the initial piece of advice I gave my new stepdaughter, and it is noteworthy for being the only advice I've ever given to a teenager that was listened to. "That's not bright enough!" she protested in the paint store. "My room is too dark! I want it bright and sunny!" When I was younger and unpracticed—in other words, when you were living at home—I would have said, "Buy it. Go ahead, sleep for the next three years inside a rotten egg yolk." To Caroline, I said, in honeyed tones, "Why don't we buy a teensy bit of each color and go home and paint itty-bitty swatches on the wall." We did; at home, her choice was a screaming, headache lemon, and my selection—which appeared pathetically pallid at the store was—yes!—bright and sunny. So it is with life, my dear. What appears funny, sentimental, individualistic out there in the world may be a screaming headache when it comes home. And it *will* come home.

Stress is not caused by overwork.

We're the daughters and granddaughters and nieces of the women who uprooted their lives and came over or across or around to a new land, a new culture. Women who, once here and often as teenagers, married, had children, and with their husbands, started ranches and farms and businesses, worked in the fields and the factories, raised chickens and vegetables and contributions for the church, took in crippled Uncle Harry, and baked a pie every day. After their husbands left them or died, they sewed to pay the bills, sang in the choir, preserved quince jelly and bread-and-butter pickles—and they still found an hour every afternoon to sit quietly and crochet. Not one of them ever said, "Oh, Agatha, I'm so stressed out."

The twenty-two extra hours you worked last week is not the cause of your stress. Stress is caused by a conflict in values: the conference during which you were asked to falsify data on the affirmative action report or the minute it took for your manager to tell you that those twenty-two salaried hours did not mean you could take Monday morning off to go to Nordstrom's shoe sale.

Of course you want to have a baby.
You're 27.

The wave isn't subtle: you'll be sitting in a
meeting, svelte and hip and on-the-money and
without warning you'll feel a tiny hand clasp
over your index finger. The biological clock is a
tidy idea; the reality is more like a neutron
bomb: your body is intact and your psyche's in
chaos.

You won't believe this; I didn't either.
When I was 23, I was approached at a company
party by my boss's wife, who asked me about
my "plans." "Plans" was a euphemism for getting

married and having children—it was not anticipated that young women would be contemplating running for Congress or updating their résumés. "I'm not going to have children," I said (yes, I said that, and, at the time, I meant it, so stop making that face and listen). She laughed and said, "That's right, you're not 27 yet."

I'll show you, I thought, furious. I worked and networked and progressed up the editorial ladder, learning my craft, loving my job, and watching disinterestedly as my friends had babies. Then I turned 27 and was overcome with an obsession to breed, slowed somewhat by the facts that I was no longer married and full-time employment was critical to the well-being of my increasing number of creditors.

Times have changed, I realize; however, I'm not talking social tolerance, I'm talking *my grandchildren*. For heaven's sake, find yourself a wonderful man, have a fairy-tale wedding, and get pregnant. I was liberated and what did it get me? A liberated son and a liberated daughter and a hushed backyard with a rusting swing set.

Clout goes with the position, not the person.

When it was my responsibility to choose who would be on the cover of a national magazine, my phone calls were returned faster than the speed of light. When I left to start a struggling company, 90 percent of my Rolodex fell through the cracks in the sidewalk of fame. We are, indeed, accomplished women with a carefully constructed network of professional contacts and friends—and it is intriguing to discover, if your signature is no longer at the bottom of a paycheck, who belongs to which category.

Stop smoking, dammit.

1. What is the point of shelling out a week's
    pay on specially blended cream from a
    Parisian cosmetician if you're going to
    inhale toxic chemicals that suck the
    moisture right out of your pores?

2. To say nothing of the wrinkles—including
    those corrugated lines over your mouth that
    drain off your lipstick in red rivulets—that
    will have everyone thinking you're *my*
    mother in ten years.

3. Your clothes—those high-styled natural
   fibers you're so fond of—carry the
   permanent fragrance of a truck-stop diner.

4. I can't quit unless you do.

Share.

One gloriously sunny Sunday afternoon, I
allowed myself to be dragged to the annual
meeting of the historical society, where we were
served a dreadful broccoli-and-chicken hot dish
and subjected to a rambling and disorganized
after-lunch lecture. Boredom had pushed me to
the brink of near-hysteria when the speaker
ended with this story:

A colleague of his, he said, had been the
sole heir of a great-aunt's treasures—china,
silver, photographs, antique furniture, linens—
to the exclusion of the other members of a large,

extended family. Believing everyone should have pieces of his or her heritage, the heiress broke up the sets of Limoges and passed around the place settings. She divided up the silver, the linens, the furniture; she duplicated the photographs, mounted them in annotated albums, and gave one to each family.

In October 1991, as she visited in another city, her house was melted to a moonscape in the Oakland Hills fire. "She lost everything she had," the speaker said. "Only what was given away was saved."

Only what we give away—knowledge, skills, wisdom—will be saved. Mentoring, not fame, is what ensures our immortality. Success is often portrayed as a race—and it is, but it is a relay, not an individual event. We grasp the baton and go as far and as fast as we can before handing off to a runner we cheer to improve the pace. And on and on . . . until we reflect on our efforts and measure our achievements by the laurels of our successors.

Forgive your friends.

Fifteen years ago, an exciting, kind, and funny woman who had been a loving friend for two decades committed an act I thought was underhanded. Imagine my horror and disgust! A self-centered decision on the part of a so-called friend! Despite a year of overtures on her part, I didn't speak to her again. Now she's gone, and if I ever was right, I have the honor of still being right. Often, a whole week goes by when I don't miss her.

Proof I wasn't a pothead: I can remember
your name from one sentence to the next
and it doesn't take me ninety minutes to
peel a potato.

When the poet W. H. Auden wrote of a "low,
dishonest decade" he was referring to the '30s,
to an era when nations lied to other nations,
and people lied to other people. Had he lived,
he could have recycled the phrase for the low,
dishonest '70s—an era when people lied to
themselves. Marijuana? No problemo, until your
epiphany the day you run into your old lab
partner from organic chemistry and she's

washing dishes in the hospital cafeteria and whispering "I hear you" to the walls. You're young and attractive. You may not need short-term memory, intellectual energy, motivation, and a sound immune system—unless the day comes when both your eyelids *and* your boobs droop—and you can't recall why either matters. Then you may wish you hadn't inhaled.

The call is not always for us.

The inner voice that guides our decisions is often acting in the interest of another. I *knew* there was a reason I was supposed to go to that New Year's Eve party, so I went, although I wanted to stay home and reread the part where Anna Karenina throws herself under the train. And what happened? Nothing. Unmemorable conversations; more names I needn't know; lousy food. What was that vibe about, I wondered? Three years later, I got a birth announcement from a stranger who wrote, "I'm the woman who corrected your pronunciation of 'Karenina,' and I married the Russian lit professor who overheard my pronunciation and corrected *me*. Keep up the good work."

Nature wastes nothing, including our time.

It takes a tough woman to cook a tender chicken.

[*Monday morning; an elevator in a New York City office building.*] I'm talking to Ann, a co-worker who is an excellent writer and editor, and an insightful art critic, a graduate of the first Princeton class to admit women. I mention this for credibility: we often talk about subjects other than recipes. Nevertheless, on this particular morning, she was giving me the instructions for what she had named Montauk Chicken. "After you add the cilantro and the ginger, you marinate it in yogurt, overnight if possible. That's the secret. The next day, add lemon juice. . . . " Her voice trailed off as we became aware of the two pinstriped gentlemen in the car with us. They were giving each other The Look that meant: "We're serious executives here, dedicating our lives to business excellence and personal success. Why must we be subjected to domestic prattling on our turf?"

Ann and I stopped talking and began staring at the flashing floor numbers. Ah, I thought, a career tip: kitchen chit-chat is not for the upwardly mobile wannabe. Best to leave the house at home.

[*Later that same day; a commuter train to*

Connecticut.] Three men, one of them an elevator companion from earlier in the day, were seated, briefcases on laps, no doubt well-deserved gin-and-tonics in hand. They were engaged in an intense debate. "No, you shouldn't spread it without checking the pH! The level of acidity relates directly to the type and amount you'll need." "I put it on once without checking, and you're absolutely right, Charlie. I had patches of brown, patches of green. Helluva mess." "Can I borrow your spreader this year?"

Hmmm. A corollary: chicken is not a power subject; the lawn is.

[*A Monday morning three weeks later; the elevator.*] Two yellow-suspendered masters of the universe were in an urgent discussion. I recognized one of them from the train. "Hi, Charlie," I said, and then—the quick student—"How's the lawn surviving this heat?" Charlie glanced my way and mumbled the minimal response, then continued his purposeful conversation: "After the coals are red hot, I throw on the chips, and add the chicken. Quickly. This is after it's marinated overnight in yogurt, of course. That's the secret."

I don't want to know everything that I demand you tell me.

Our cat, Ethel, who accompanied me through two marriages and a cross-country relocation, died at the age of fifteen on the same day we discovered the body of your hamster, Judy. Ethel, an excellent hunter in her day, was credited with the kill. So as not to interfere with your mourning, I hid my delight that Ethel had not gone gentle into that good night; for years, the thought that she was vital to the end was a comfort. When I sold the house in New York and cleaned out the attic, I found your seventh-grade diary. Sorry to say, I read it: I justified this by determining that sixteen years after you were twelve, what could be the harm? And what had you confided, in an April entry? "Judy died today. She starved to death because I didn't remember to feed her. I blamed Ethel."

There may be a couple of other secrets you've kept over the years—just a guess—and although I'm dying to know, don't tell me; it'll kill me.

*Never hesitate to employ the airhead
defense.*

You have a brain, but that's no excuse for
flaunting it. In matters of frivolous legal hassling
("My client claims the fourth branch from the
left of the pink blossoms on your dogwood tree
is hanging over her fence. . . . "), a letter from a
lawyer doesn't mean you need to hire one. The
standard game is this: You receive a firm, mildly
threatening letter on intimidating embossed
stationery. It is expected that you will engage in
the game by hiring your own mouthpiece: a
match of legal tennis would then be established

at astonishingly high hourly rates. This is rarely necessary: better to write a flagrantly irresponsible reply, thereby indicating you are indigent and emotionally unstable. This will unnerve the attorney. Attorneys only enjoy playing with other attorneys—precious few

 are willing to enter into adversarial relationships with ordinary folks. Chances are good that the client—who intends to win by draining your cash reserves on professional fees—will back off.

Warning: This counsel from Mom's Legal Aid is valid only for civil harassments. If you are

arrested for grand theft auto while driving a
newly purchased Toyota that the previous three
owners neglected to register (a particularly
sensitive event of my own), retain a lawyer fast.
Don't use your one phone call to cancel your
manicure.

Revisit decisions.

I decided once and for all to dye my hair plum wine, to double-major in French and history, to go into corporate public relations, to relocate to Chicago, to marry that man I met in the lounge of the Sheraton-Dallas, to drive a '41 Mercury, to apply to the Yale School of Divinity, to take a course in cake decorating, to refinish the piano myself. Will people think you're flaky if you keep changing your mind? Yes. So what.

When someone dies, cook.

One Friday night we came home from dinner at
an Italian restaurant and the telephone rang
before I could take my coat off. It was a man I
didn't know, a friend's neighbor. I was
processing his name, putting it in the right
category, as he was saying, "I hate to be the one
to tell you this . . . " and then my mind jumped
to a dozen possibilities in the nanosecond
before he said, " . . . killed herself last night."

Numbly, I did what I'd been taught to do:
I baked a ham and scalloped potatoes; I fixed a
strawberry Jell-O salad with canned fruit. When

the food was prepared, I packed it carefully in
the car and phoned my mother. "I'm going over
there now," I said. "What do I say?" "Don't break
down," she said, "unless they do."

There is nothing to say;
there is no language for death.
Hold each other and let the tears
shake your bodies; eat; tell stories; laugh
without guilt. Most of all, forgive the dead, and
forgive yourself: We never love as much as we
should, but we all love as much as we can.

Know the difference between power and control.

In the spring of '92, Ferndale, my hometown, was the epicenter of three major earthquakes in eighteen hours. Pam relayed the bad news to me on the other side of the country. "Everyone's chimney is down, the front of the grocery store fell into the street, the cupboards flew open and the dishes and canned goods crashed onto the floor. The Red Cross has set up an emergency shelter at the Fairgrounds. Nancy and I went down to check it out. Nancy's house has collapsed. Red Cross volunteers were passing out box lunches; Nancy and I stood around, looking for ways to help. Suddenly, it hit me. I said, "Nancy, take a sandwich. We're the victims here. We don't always have to be the ones who *make* the sandwiches. Sometimes, it's our turn to *take* the sandwiches."

There is a rhythm to giving and receiving; it is the rhythm of control and power. Power— the rush of being filled with creative energy, with open enthusiasm—comes after we give up control, when we relinquish our insistence on making the sandwiches and simply, gratefully, take one.

Relax; other people are not obsessed with your problems.

I was terrified to tell my mother that my marriage was ending in divorce ("After that beautiful wedding?"). I was certain it would destroy her. After weeks of anxiety, I flew home for a face-to-face announcement. I had the opener and the ensuing explanations memorized. She met me at the airport, forty miles away, and it was thirty-six miles of small talk ("What have you done to your hair?") before I was able to burst out with the news.

"Al and I are getting a divorce," I said.

And she said, "Oh, honey, I'm so sorry. That's a shame. Do his parents know? They're such lovely people."

I started to sob. "I feel like crying, too," she said. "When we get home, you can help me make a rhubarb cream pie. I've already got a nice pork roast in the oven."

After dinner, we sat in the kitchen and talked: she was worried about why the dog was chewing up the recliner.

Shop in old classified ads.

With the first dollar down, with the first "yes!,"
the seller often cancels his ads for the '56 sports
car, the five-room apartment with an ocean
view, the Sheraton sideboard—and then the deal
falls through a week later. That's when to
respond ("Hello, do you still have that Alfa
Romeo for sale?"). Bonus: even if the item they
were selling is gone, they may have heard from
other potential sellers who saw the ad ("I've got
an Alfa that sounds like yours; let me know if
you get your price").

P.S. Those of us who are not adept at hiring the right people agree that old want ads are excellent secret sources for the job seeker. Scour the newspapers from a couple of months back and apply for the intriguing jobs: ("Saw your ad for an apprentice taxidermist while doing research on collagen implants. If the position is open, I'd be delighted to be considered.") Well, the position has been filled, but the fillee has turned out to be the bride of Godzilla, and yes, we'd be delighted to consider you.

Fail fearlessly.

Who's Who sent me a congratulatory letter ("You have been chosen . . . !") with an attached questionnaire. The implication was clear: if the answers on the form were satisfactory, I'd be included in the forty-fourth edition of that worthy publication (which I would then be expected to purchase). The questions covered the usual categories for determining the measure of success: degrees, achievements, awards, publications, honors, elective offices, scholarly recognitions. I didn't find out if my responses would have qualified me as a *Who*: I didn't return the form. One line for marital history? Insufficient space for children's surnames? No space for the "I coulda been a contender" stories, no queries about struggles, defeats, setbacks, and downright disasters. What's the point of people knowing you're a *Who* if they don't know *Why* you chose that path or *How* you traveled it? We are defined by our failures: *Who* we are is how we overcame the six D's in college; it is the humility we acquired from being fired, the character we developed after the divorce, the gratitude we realized when we were broke.

*Expect an occasional punishment to
ridiculously outweigh the crime.*

"It isn't fair," you will complain. "All I did was
double-park." Yes, and your car was impounded
and later vandalized in the tow lot, to the
annoyance of your insurance company, which
promptly canceled your policy, leaving you in
the high-risk category, which you couldn't
afford, so you lost your license and then—
because you couldn't drive to work—your job,
and that's why your electricity was shut off. We
can see this far down the road because we've
been there. That's why we repeat, "Better drive

around the block again and find a legal spot to park," after you've cried, "Lighten up! I'll only be a minute!"

A silly old song by the Kingston Trio, "The Tijuana Jail," describes the woes of a carefree traveler who commits a minor legal infraction and is sentenced to life in a Mexican prison. Under the final refrain, he mutters, "This all has sure been a lesson to me." There are some lessons we don't need to learn.

Make it through the night.

Cortisol—the enzyme that coats our nerve endings and gives us the ability to cope—drips for twenty-two hours a day. It stops dripping between four and six in the morning, which is why it's darkest before dawn and why, in hospitals, those hours are the most common for people to die. Does it help to know this? Of course not. The reason I can't sleep, I convince myself, is that I left those black suede shoes in a hotel room in Denver and if I could ever find another pair like them, which I won't, it would cost five hundred dollars, which I can't justify spending on evening clothes, although, strike me dead, I should have nice things after how hard I've worked. Before e-mail, we felt tragically isolated. Now, we can go on-line and read frantic messages clocked at 4:42 A.M. from people we assumed sane. Save yourself the embarrassed 7:00 A.M. apology—"Ignore my e-mail. I don't know what came over me"—and try to hang in there until the cortisol resumes its drip.

Temper your ambitious urgency.

One summer, I hired two newly graduated
college women to intern at the magazine. It was
a contest, of sorts: there was a single permanent
opening on the staff budgeted for the fall. While
both interns were capable, one was an
exceptional writer and had a keen sense of
"what's hot and what's not"; by July, it was clear
she was the candidate for the full-time position.
Then, abruptly, she came into my office and
asked if we could speak privately; as soon as the
door was closed, she announced she was
quitting. "I didn't get an education to Xerox

manuscripts," she began, and then she went on to list her many skills, of which we were well aware. Denouncing my failure to provide her with vast opportunities, she said, "I've been here six weeks already, and as far as I can see, my career is going nowhere." She left for greener pastures. In September, we hired the remaining intern—a woman who is today working far up the masthead on a magazine in New York. The impatient one? Who knows?

Develop bifocal vision.

Vision is not visualization. Visualization is pattern thinking: If I see myself giving a speech in Rochester wearing a pink suit, I may actually purchase the airline tickets and pack the suit. Far-sighted vision, a view of the horizon, is spiritually informed; it is a picture of the magnificent goals—the goals which are not for ourselves and which we cannot achieve by ourselves or in our lifetime: alleviating hunger, fostering peace, reducing illiteracy, restoring the earth, preventing disease, encouraging the arts, rejoicing in diversity.

The lower section of the bifocals is for nearsighted vision: our focus on the present. As Jeanne DuPrau wrote in *The Earth House*, "There is nothing to fear in this moment, and this is the only real moment there is."

Tomorrow, next week, five years from now—convenient frames we have manufactured to fence in the chaos of time. All that is real is this moment, *now*, and the hope on the horizon.

Laugh loudly and the hell with it.

We were told: you would be such a pretty girl if you could keep your mouth shut, if you would smile more, hold your tongue, keep your hair shiny, get your teeth straightened, walk as though you had a book balanced on your head, shoulders back—you're not leaving the house in that outfit!—don't chew gum in public, and clean up your language.

I'm telling you: if you keep your mouth shut, you *will* be a pretty girl—but you won't be a vital, exciting, self-assured woman. (Okay, I'd cool it on the gum.)

A good man is not hard to find, Part II.

He listens to bluegrass.

In the mix of America's folk lyrics and the virtuoso of the musicians on a panoply of stringed instruments, you have an intellectual and a sentimentalist with a sense of humor and an absence of classism. You also have a man who will stay up all night practicing the mandolin and eating squirrel stew with strangers; it's a trade-off.

Hair: the front line of mental health.

We are warned not to make decisions based
solely on being frightened or alone; fear and
loneliness are always with us. I'd like to add:
don't pull the plug without a great haircut. Get
your nails done. Indulge in a pedicure and a
facial. A massage may be in order. Get your
brows and legs waxed. Ponder an herbal wrap.
Read the trash talk in fashion magazines. Dress
 up; meet an irreverent friend for
Thai food. Then, drop-dead
gorgeous and full of sass, decide
if you want to quit that job, leave

that husband, drop out of school, sell the house, or enter the convent.

Four hours before she died, my ninety-two-year-old aunt sent her neighbor home from the hospital with instructions to return with her brush and her lipstick. Characteristically, she had her priorities in order.

Envy is not knowing the whole story.

Shakespeare ("Wishing me like to one more rich in hope . . . desiring this man's art and that man's scope . . . ") was jealous, so it's understandable if you, too, lose perspective. Just keep in mind that a particularly fanciful game of the cosmos is to grant our wishes ("Be careful what you pray for," the old warning goes, "you may get it."). I've made a list, in chronological order, of what I have coveted since the first grade:

- naturally curly hair
- straight teeth
- boobs
- a record player
- big allowances
- a cute boyfriend
- a driver's license
- the nerve to take trigonometry
- matching sweaters and socks
- a fraternity serenade
- a hi-fi
- trips to conventions
- by-lines

- whopping salaries (more than $15,000!)
- backpacking in Europe
- babies
- happy marriages
- clean, decorated houses
- husbands who dance
- successful entrepreneurial businesses
- theater tickets
- a flat stomach
- fashion flair
- *humongous* incomes
- an amazing sound system

Naturally curly hair? At last! But it's gray. Humongous incomes? How hard are you willing to work? A clean house? Why? Husbands who dance? Yes.

Balance your checkbook, not your life.

Juggle your priorities? I never did; I stopped
trying. Twenty years ago, at the Comedy Club
on Sunset Strip, I saw a juggler—a young man
who, alone in the spotlight, tossed a head of
lettuce, a plucked chicken, and an orange M&M
in a perfect, continuous circle. I thought, Wow.
(That was the '70s; if it had been the '80s, I
would have thought, Whoa. In the '90s, I would
have said, "What an unambiguous metaphor.")
Wow, I thought: a head of lettuce represents my
financial problems ("challenges"); the naked,
limp chicken is certainly a symbol for the

84

powers that be; and the M&M is the spot of joy we hope will occasionally pop up. The three items were juggled in perfect rhythm, each having an equal turn in the light. "I can make it," I thought, "no matter how tough office politics and relationship grief, no matter how broke I am or how exhausted or tense—sweet times are in the loop."

Does anyone have it all? Now and then. Forever? No. Balance and order exist only in freeze frame.

Let the creek meander.

Restoring the fish habitat at the ranch, I told the conservationist I wanted to straighten out the creek. "Why?" he asked. "In a few years, it will wind along again. Creeks want to meander."

So do our hearts and imaginations. We can develop five-year goals and five-day schedules, yet we can't see over the horizon of this afternoon. If what we plan for Tuesday morning actually happens, it's a miracle. Nevertheless, we go on, day after day, planning as if this week, if we're *sincerely* focused, will come together. Our soul connects us to the

natural world and skews toward chaos,
splashing over the stones, flooding with the
winter rains, stagnating under the fallen alders.

    We need a thin layer of organization—the
minimum required to keep our health insurance
current and the oil changed—over a stream of
free-flowing passion.

Enjoy anonymity while you can.

One afternoon, I caught an early train from
Grand Central to Connecticut and sat in the
five-togethers, a group of seats occupied in the
rush hour by bridge players. Scrunched up
against the window, working on a needlepoint
bluebird, was another woman professionally
attired (and professionally tired). We nodded
wordlessly, and I opened my newspaper. Before
the train left the station, we were joined by
two men with overstuffed attaché cases from
which they each pulled a yellow legal pad.

"What've you got?" asked one. "We're going to have to file Chapter 11 on Monday, and I don't need to tell you what that will do to the stock," replied the other. "We have tomorrow then? I'll let George know." I shot a sidelong glance at the needlepointer; she caught my look and raised her eyebrows in a "I can't believe what I'm hearing" message. The men continued to share privileged information from their respective clients: the company in trouble and the significant investor. When the train pulled into Stamford, one of the attorneys rose to debark, saying, "Paul, thanks. I'm glad we had a chance to talk privately."

When I was a child, I wished I was invisible. Now, I am a woman. Pouf! My wish has come true.

A good man . . . Part III.

He rides merry-go-rounds, holding on to the
pole with one hand and reaching out for you
with his free hand—and he rides them wherever
he finds them: child-filled sparklers in Disney
World, grandiose antiques in Santa Cruz,
abandoned hulks in the wilds of Wilkes-Barre.

The attributes are obvious: a sense of play,
wonder, romance. Hopping spontaneously on a
carousel, face to the wind, is a man-child you
can love. Just pray he knows when to get off.

Insomnia is compulsory education.

Biology curricula aside, your body is run by
stern gnomes who work three eight-hour shifts,
and those fellows on the ten-to-six overnight are
rigid and humorless (you'll learn this if you eat
a massive slab of prime rib at an ungodly
hour—the third shift doesn't do digestion;
they'll leave the job for the day team). The way I
see it, the job of the third shift is the same as
office maintenance crews: put everything away
in its proper place, empty wastebaskets,
vacuum, air out the rooms; the way the workers
see it, their job is to go through the

wastebaskets, read the stuff on the desk, re-run the videos of the day, and comment. They find unpaid bills, overlooked clues, evidence of denial and procrastination, remnants of broken promises—and they drag us through dreams that resemble paper-bag skits, stories invented from the dregs of the day ("Whaddaya wanna do with these lines from 'Don't Be Cruel'? Do they belong in the same basket as the reminder to buy nonfat milk? Where did you put the telephone bill? Didn't that woman in Safeway look like a girl you knew in college?")

All right, here's the dream: You're in a market talking to Elvis on a cell phone. You try to buy milk and because you can't find your wallet, you're arrested by a woman you knew in college. She doesn't recognize you naked. ("Why am I naked?" "So you'll know it's a dream.") If the guys on graveyard get stuck, they wake us up ("We can't do another thing until you clean up this mess.").

We can sleep with medication, but we won't get the mess cleaned up and we'll have a third shift run by druggies.

A good man . . . Part IV.

He pays his bills.

A contract with the gas company (I'll give you money if you heat my house) is as much a measure of integrity as an emotional contract to love and cherish. Watch for the clues: if he keeps impeccable records for his tax deductions and stiffs the neighbor kid who watered his plants, run for your life.

Score no unnecessary points.

Let me fling up a bunch of metaphoric clay
pigeons and shoot them out of the sky:

1. Take no prisoners: A version of the
    "scorched earth" philosophy, which tells us
    to create for our adversaries utter defeat
    and total humiliation. It was that post–
    World War I strategy that turned the War to
    End All Wars into a pre-game warm-up for
    the Holocaust. But don't let the facts get in
    the way of a justification for Notre Dame

wiping out Southeast Missouri State 85–0
in a rousing victory for alumni fund-raisers.

2. Winning is the only thing: Another major
   tenet of Western ethics brought to us by
   that bastion of philosophic thinking, the
   National Football League. Actually, there are
   quite a number of things more important
   than winning: Awe, beauty, camaraderie,
   devotion, energy, faith, grace, health,
   integrity, judgment, kindness, loyalty,
   merriment, neighborliness, opportunity,
   purpose, quietude, recreation, spontaneity,

tradition, understanding, vigor, wisdom,
xhuberance (okay, give me a break),
youthfulness, zeal—to run, for starters,
through a child's alphabet of virtues.

3. To the victor belong the spoils: This is the
   negative flip side of the negotiator's axiom
   that tells us to always leave something on
   the table. Be honorable: Don't demand *all*
   that is due you; never strip the dignity from
   an adversary; never exact eye-for-an-eye
   vengeance. The whole world is endangered
   by Hatfields and McCoys, Crips and

Bloods, Tutsis and Hutus, Lancasters and
Yorks, Serbs and Croats, and all the Irish
(I'm Irish; I can say this; hold your fire).

Once upon a time, in the olden days,
students were rewarded with rallies and banners
and picnics and trophies for sportsmanship. The
ideal was to teach human beings to compete
with respect. We've lost that old-fashioned mark
of character, and, despite what folks might want
to believe, we didn't lose it in the decaying
streets of our inner cities, we lost it in the halls
of military decision makers who glorified
machine-gun massacres of fleeing foot soldiers

from low-flying helicopters, and we lost it in the sanctuaries of congregations that, upon hearing this news, arose and sang "America the Beautiful."

Restrain yourself from looking underneath anything.

Dripping oil? Lost change in the sofa? A funny noise in the crawlspace? Is that *fat* along my jawbone? What did he mean when he said he loved me? I wonder how long it's been since I vacuumed behind the dust ruffle? Shepherd's pie is—mashed potatoes on top of *what?*

Do we really want to know? Knowledge may be power; illusion is the cornerpost of sanity.

*As soon as you learn the game, the rules
will change.*

We hung around the elementary school
playground on long afternoons, watching the
boys play pick-up basketball and hoping that
Duane's little brother would have to go home
early and we would be reluctantly allowed to
substitute. On Saturdays, in Carol's driveway, we
practiced dribbling, shooting lay-ups, guarding
and rebounding; by the time we were permitted
into a game, we were *ready*. Whiz! Zap! Three
rebounds, two steals, and six points later, the

game was halted. "From now on," the oldest
boy solemnly declared, "girls have to shoot from
behind the curb."

You will never regret NOT sleeping with someone.

The might-have-beens give us delicious flashbacks of bittersweet nostalgia unscarred by humilities of the flesh and sorrows of the heart—to say nothing of revisionist histories ("I watched you at every rehearsal and wished you were mine." Or, my personal favorite: "I carried those two round-trip tickets to Tobago in my wallet for fifteen years.") The never-should-have-been hangs around the edges of our minds like a fragment of a seedy country song, a song that doesn't let us forget that sex can have as much to do with revenge and boredom as it does with love. And it's not usually the guy you regret: it's the version of you that went with him.

Don't look back: learning a lot from Lot's wife.

We want a second chance, on our own terms, on our own schedules. Opportunity doesn't work that way: if an angel grabs you by the hand and pulls you out of an exploding city, get a move on. We know why Mrs. Lot turned around: she missed her neighbors; in the rush, she'd forgotten her favorite pots; she wanted a final good-bye. Lot's wife was changed into a pillar of salt, and we will be, too, from the salt of our own tears. "I should never have left L.A. What would that stock in Disney be worth today? I wish I'd taken that job. Why wasn't I a better mother? Where did the money go?"

A second chance, or a third, or a fourth, requires a complete commitment: head into a new land unburdened by disappointments, empowered by experience, and eyes forward.

Keep your eye on the ball.

I have a nameplate on my desk. It's one that was standard thirty or forty years ago—a rounded wooden base with a horizontal slit that holds a strip of black plastic with white letters. The nameplate was given to me after the editor on my first "real job" invited me to lunch (I was going out to lunch! On business!). After the meal, Bob asked, "How's the work going? Is there anything you need?" (The purpose of that question, indeed, of that lunch, had been to announce I was getting a $50-a-month raise. I learned this years later.) "I love my job!" I said, ever the cool negotiator. And then, my cheeks reddening, "Except for one thing." "What is it?" "Well . . . I am the only person in the office who doesn't have a nameplate on their desk." "I'll take care of that in the morning," he said.

The next day, the black nameplate was on my desk. Bob had found it in his garage. The white letters read: "Claude E. Spriggs/Licensed Real Estate Broker." I had asked for an image, and I had been given one. The raise was postponed.

Fast.

The original sacrifice was to go without food in the days when food was scarce. Now, we look forward to fasting; it's a foolproof way to stay on our diets. Want real suffering? Try communications fasting: no telephone, fax, e-mail, television, books, radio, CDs, visits, newspapers, magazines, letters, videos, computer games. Go cold turkey. Shut out the voices of the world and submit to utter solitude. Expect to be surprised by the new voice you'll hear: it's your heart, clamoring for attention.

A good man . . . Part V.

He asks for directions.

And follows them. The comfort with
which he is able to appear fallible in the eyes of
an eighteen-year-old gas station attendant is a
significant clue to his self-confidence and a clear
predictor of how many dinner parties you will
arrive at punctually and still in love. Look
carefully, however; there are just nine of these
men extant in the Western Hemisphere, and I
have one of them.

Exorcize the demons of common sense.

The voices came to me the day before I resigned
from the so-called world's greatest job; I called
them The Furies. I was a literature major, and
these voices sounded to me as I supposed the
chorus of witches sounded to Orestes. "You
can't quit!" shrieked The Furies. "You have it
made! Money, bonuses, medical insurance,
profit-sharing. Look at this office! A view of
three rivers! You have an assistant and a
secretary, limos greet your plane, Jane Pauley
meets you for lunch. And best of all," the voices
dropping, conspiratorially, "you can do this job

in your sleep. You can make the early train home, be with your family. Don't start over," the voices pleaded. "We remember what it was like when you started that company in California, and we never want to work that hard again."

Ah, the temptations we must resist. Chances are you won't have to struggle with horned satyrs for your indomitable spirit. We are too sophisticated for such encounters. Our demons disguise themselves as common sense, as practical solutions. They come chanting slogans about growing up, acting your age, settling down; they remind us of what others will think of us; they taunt us with the possibility of failure and ridicule. Medieval or modern, the results are the same: we stifle the dream, our inner sense of mission, the call for selfless service, our urge for adventure. Switch by switch, we walk around the factory of our soul and turn off the lights.

A good man . . . Part VI.

He will repeat a conversation word for word,
nuance for nuance.

You have to do the training: it's a special
course called "He said/She said." The results are
worth the effort. No more: "Did you talk to Joe?
How was his weekend in Aruba with Lisa?"
"Fine, I guess."

The longer the story, the bigger the lie.

The answer to "Why are you late?" is "Traffic" and not what I said when I was nineteen minutes tardy to fifth grade (obliterating any chance of my winning the competition for a perfect arrival/attendance record): "The calves broke out, and I had to help my mother chase them down the lane, and then the cow came after them, breaking down the fence by the chicken house and chickens scattered and the cat took off." I've had similar answers to my questions: "What do you need the money for?"

"Where were you?" "When may we expect payment?" "Do you love me?"

Remember, when asked, "Who was that lady I saw you with last night?" the vaudevillian's response was, "That was no lady, that was my wife"—*not* "That was no lady, that was the woman I was telling you about who has the uncle in Bulgaria with no work permit and six days to live unless he can find a liver donor with his blood type—what's that rare kind? AB negative—and the nearest donor is in Saõ Paulo, unbelievable, right? She speaks Portuguese, fortunately, and I ran into her coming out of the Berlitz school a week ago and she asked me to help because of my expertise in, you know, inventory management, which, surprisingly, has an unusual connection with liver disease...."

Life is a journey?

Refrigerator magnets and greeting cards and
smile-faced post-its stuck to your pillow by
people too shy to hug proclaim the eternal
truth, that life is a journey. We women believe
this, uh-huh, we brag about how spontaneous
we are at taking trips: We stop for ice cream
when we want to, stay overnight at bed-and-
breakfasts down by the river, and explore back
roads to antique shops. Not like taking a trip
with a man, who doesn't pretend life is a
journey, a man who is desperately eager to make
time to get where he didn't want to go in the

first place, a man who, although you're blue-faced and cross-legged and begging to stop at the next gas station, merely shakes his head and says, "I told you not to have that cup of coffee back in Louisville!"

If we're so civilized about taking trips, what happens to us on the real journey? Why are we jumping up and down in the back seat the whole way, shouting, "Are we there yet? Are we *there* yet? How much farther?" Susan Taylor, the funny and wise editor-in-chief of *Essence* magazine, warns against the rush to get "there." "You know when you're 'there'?" she asks. "You're lying in that long wooden box and everyone is standing around looking at you, nodding their heads and murmuring, 'She was a *good* woman.'"

Do the right thing, even if it's for the wrong reasons.

Shortly after becoming editor-in-chief of a woman's magazine, I began a reign of, if not exactly terror, certainly vengeance. My inherited staff remained loyal to my beloved predecessor, whom I could never emulate (my thrift shop rabbit coat juxtaposed against her floor-length sable was an apt symbol). Gratuitously, I issued executive orders to emphasize the change in regimes, grasping every potential situation, no matter how petty, to assert my tenuous power. (To appreciate this story, you must accept that nothing I did was generous in spirit; my actions were motivated entirely by a bruised ego.) One afternoon, I noticed an assistant wheeling a dolly filled with books down the hall. The dolly held about three hundred titles of new books; they had been shipped to us by publishers seeking reviews. I asked the assistant where she was going. She said she was taking them to the Strand, a used bookstore, to sell them (it's not legal to sell review copies of books, by the way; that's another issue). The proceeds, she explained, were to be used, as they always had been, for a staff party.

"No longer!" I announced. "Things are different around here now. We'll be doing, uh, something else." "What?" In a flash of pseudo-noblesse oblige, I said, "We're giving them to the library at the women's prison. Pack them up for UPS." Then I called the Bedford Hills Correctional Facility, a maximum-security prison for women fifty miles north, and asked the desk officer for the mailing address. That afternoon and once or twice a month thereafter for five years, we shipped cartons of new books upstate. Each shipment was acknowledged by a pleasant thank-you letter from the prison librarian.

Many years passed, and now I was the

owner of an unsuccessful company that I ran out of my house. My pastor, noting that lack of business had granted me lots of free time, suggested that I accompany him to the Bedford Hills prison and help him present a series of seminars to a group of inmates. We arrived forty minutes early to clear the security process for me, the newcomer. To our surprise, we zipped through. Inside, with nothing to do (a familiar complaint to the regulars), I said, "I'd like to see the library. I used to know who the librarian was." A guard pointed to a doorway down the hall. "We've always had the same librarian; she's in there now. Go ahead."

The library was impressive: airy rooms with walls lined with thousands of books, racks of current magazines and newspapers, audio books, music tapes, study tables. A plainly dressed older woman, whom I later learned was a nun, was standing by a desk. I introduced myself and started to mention my former position when she interrupted me.

"Ladies!" she cried ("Ladies!"—the institutional euphemism for correctional residents). "Come in here! Here is the woman who started our library!" Stunned, I stood, my pastor at my side, and listened to this story.

The nun had been assigned to start a

library at the Bedford Hills prison and was given a room—dimly lit with filthy windows, filled with broken and scarred wooden tables, a floor of peeling linoleum; a crew of inmates; and no budget. In the corner of the room were two boxes of books: Reader's Digest Condensed Books and thirty copies of a junior high school social studies text dating from 1960. She gathered her workers, and they began to wash windows, cover the tables with Contac paper, clean the blackboard, scrub the woodwork. They put the dusty old books in the dumpster; the nun said, "Our library is going to have real books." They mopped the floor and, with help from a volunteer, painted the walls. In four days, the room was cheerful and clean. And empty. At the end of the fourth day, when the inmates were back in their rooms, the nun sat down at a table and put her head in her hands. "O Lord," she said, "where are we going to find the books?" The next morning, UPS arrived with three hundred new books from *Savvy* magazine.

Don't wait for the purity of your motives to do the right thing. It's acceptable to volunteer at the homeless shelter because you want to network with the banker who also volunteers there: People who need a bowl of soup aren't concerned with why you are serving them. The most noble act I may ever accomplish occurred in spite of my arrogance. The earth is so starved for nourishment it will absorb whatever we have to offer and transform even the most selfish deeds into glory if we only but aim them in the right direction.

Offices are villages, not families.

It was bound to happen; the touchy-feely '70s led right into mucho dinero for management gurus in the '80s. Dysfunctional families? We can fix that—we'll provide emotional nurturing in the workplace.

To survive the inevitable politics, think of the office as a small town—a mix of people who lead separate lives in close proximity and who must simultaneously create a community that provides for their needs and protects them against their enemies, and maintain sufficient distance to develop as effective individuals. A bit of sophomore-level economic theory wouldn't hurt here: Capitalism has, as its goal, the production of profits for investors. In other words, sweetie, there *is* a family at work, and it's not composed of friends in the home office and its regional branches—it's composed of the shareholders. The CEO on the "Nightly Business News" who's declaring that the workforce at Megalocorp, Inc., is "just one big happy family" has a prenuptial agreement, custody papers, sole executor rights, and a divorce attorney on retainer. Although your boss may be old enough to be your mother, she's not your mother, I am, and here's the difference: if anyone ever came to

me and pointed to your name on a list to be
down-sized, that person had better get fitted for
cement high-heels, if you catch my drift.

A good man . . . Part VII.

He doesn't make mayonnaise in a thunderstorm.

Or allow call-waiting to interrupt your tearful reconciliation. *The Joy of Cooking* warns us about fooling around with eggs and lemon juice and oil while the heavens are erupting with electrical fury, and our heart should warn us if a random telephone connection with the world is more important than our earnest expressions of love. "Curdle" is the word that comes to mind.

Your twenties are a Magic Slate.

The toy is a piece of treated cardboard covered with a layer of cellophane. You write with what appears to be a cuticle stick on the cellophane, pull up the cellophane, and whoosh! the writing disappears, the slate is clean, you can begin again. We bumble along in our twenties, moving from jobs, apartments, boyfriends, having our more lasting relationships with our cat and a ragged copy of *Siddhartha*. Mistakes ("I thought the deposit would have cleared by now") come and go; disasters (his old girlfriend sets fire to the car) reveal the fragile membrane that separates us from the characters in *General Hospital*. We continue to write on the Magic Slate and pull up the cellophane of forgiveness until, unexpectedly, barely into our thirties, we go to erase the slate and the words stick. The toy is damaged from overuse; traces adhere. It serves as notice that the magic has ended; we have left the free zone of trial-and-error, and we will be held accountable for what we say and what we do, today and forever.

Write letters to the living.

It's a toss-up: You can pay thousands of dollars
to learn to accept your thoughtless omissions—
or you can write thank-you notes. I've timed the
task: it would have taken me seven minutes to
write a letter to my high school English teacher
and tell her how much I appreciated her
attention, her concern, and her unpopular
efforts on my behalf. She did all the required
stuff right—gave me encouragement and
discipline in my writing, expanded my literary
horizons, rewarded creativity—and then she
went the extra mile. As the advisor to the

yearbook staff, she changed the caption ("A wiggle in her walk and a giggle in her talk") that had been submitted under my senior picture. The day the yearbooks arrived from the printers, there was a considerable stir: it was a tiny high school and everyone had been told the epigrams Linda and Lynette, the student editors, had chosen for each graduating senior—so everyone knew that mine had been altered. The paste-up was retrieved from the printer, and the culprit was revealed—in that unmistakable hand of our English teacher, a fine line was drawn through wiggle/giggle and a new phrase substituted. It said, "Small package, big person."

Big person? The serene, dignified, exacting English teacher thought I—whom the whole town agreed was merely smart-mouthed and boy-crazy—I was a *big person*? I've spent the intervening thirty-five years trying to live up to her assessment. And I would have spent an additional seven minutes writing a letter to thank her—I especially meant to do it when I heard she had retired, and, later, when I knew she was dying—but I waited, until later, when I had more time, when I could re-check her address, when I could write a meaningful letter and not a hurried note.

I'll do it now, in her memory, for all the

teachers who wonder, amidst the mountains of uncorrected papers and the sea of seemingly bored faces, if they've ever truly changed a child's life.

Thank you, Mrs. Horn.

The horse may talk.

The cliches about time—time is on our side,
time and tide wait for no man, time heals all
wounds, to everything there is a season, give it
time, haste makes waste, there's many a slip
'twixt the cup and the lip—are true. So is
"Sufficient unto the day is the evil thereof," and
the words that are written on my mother-in-
law's teapot: "Don't worry, it may never happen."

A fable tells of the court jester who
attempted to swindle the king by claiming to be
able to teach the king's horse to talk. The jester
requested, and received, two hundred pieces of

gold to perform this miracle. Six months passed, and then a year, and the horse remained speechless. The king, wisely determining he had been fooled, demanded the return of his gold; when the jester, recently accustomed to high living, was unable to return the gold, the king said, "Off with his head." "Hold on," the jester said, grasping for the quick fix, "tell you what. Spare me for another twelve months and I will guarantee you a conversational horse. If I fail, you can draw-and-quarter me in the town square—considerably more satisfying a penalty than a mere decapitation." "Okay," said the king, or "Yea, verily," or whatever kings said in fables, and the jester was given another year to fulfill his boast. "You're crackers," a palace guard commented. "Another year? How's that going to change anything?" "You never know," said the jester. "In a year, the king may be dead. Or I may be dead. Or the horse may talk."

Don't anthropomorphize machines.

The computer that spit out "This is a final disconnect notice" will not recognize you on the street. A car doesn't know it's streaked with mud. The alarm clock is callously unconcerned by whether or not we hit the snooze button six times and miss the interview. And you can learn to ignore the sarcastic remarks ("Weren't you just here?") from the refrigerator.

Listen to your own contradictions.

"I can support myself," we say proudly, and then we go to support groups, long for supportive husbands, wonder why women aren't supporting other women, demand more support from our institutions, and wear support hose. So where is it written we have to be consistent? Accept the paradox. A friend wrote, "Business is booming. I've bought a fabulous house, a new Lexus, a roomful of designer clothes, and two pieces of real jewelry. I'm so proud I've been able to provide such a good living for myself— oh, what's the matter with me? Why doesn't anyone love me enough to provide these for me? I'm tremendously satisfied with my career—why do I have to have a career? Aren't I pretty enough?" I recall an aging sugar baron who leaned over to me on the train and asked about a woman who, absent that day, was a regular commuter. "She is so beautiful," he said, "so intelligent, so charming. Why on earth is she *working*?"

We *can* support ourselves, and we want to—except when we don't want to.

Don't edit your life story.

There was an opening on the magazine for a managing editor, and the résumés poured in: the magazine was hot and the competition was fierce. In the pile was an application from a woman who'd been in town two weeks. Her previous job had been with a regional Texas magazine, and her experience rested heavily on a former career as a baker, including several years in Austria training in the art of Viennese pastry making. I called the applicant in for an interview; she had all the required attributes. Managing editors have to get up early and stay into the wee hours of the night putting a magazine "to bed"—certainly familiar working conditions for someone who was used to decorating petit fours at three A.M. Managing editors also have to be sticklers for detail, pleasing a variety of tyrannical people, in much the same way a patissier produces a wedding cake. More important, I was impressed by two other characteristics revealed in the job application: the woman had an eccentric vision and the stamina to go for it, and she had the pride to keep the cookie years on her résumé. (Few career counselors would have advised thusly; at the very least, they would have suggested she change the "baker" description to "perishable manufacturing management.") She had less magazine experience than most of the other applicants. I hired her anyway. Today, I am no longer in the magazine business; the magazine itself no longer exists; the company that owned the magazine is bankrupt—but the pastry chef from Texas is well up the masthead at *Vanity Fair,* and her sacher tortes aren't suffering, either.

Who we are, who we *really* are, the unique product of Me, is all we have to take to the market. Don't trade it for a handful of magic beans.

A good man . . . Part VIII.

He has two friends.

If he's over 30, two guys, both weird and neither of whom likes the other, is about average. We often make the mistake of wanting men to have as many friends as we do; then when they do—and they go hunting over Thanksgiving and meet on alternate Sundays for the Giants game and rush out of the house at 2 A.M. to tow Frankie's car back from Dayton—well, think about it.

Play the hand you've been dealt.

"Today is the first day of the rest of your life"
is a bit portentous; I prefer to wake up to
five-card-draw poker. Each morning, a new
hand; some days, junk; some days, a full house,
and every day, the challenge of playing that
hand to win. Bluffing, "a display of false con-
fidence" the dictionary tells us, is as valuable a
skill as the ability to restrain the giddiness of a
slam-dunk royal flush.

    Discouraged that the dealer may have
rigged the game? In 1992, an obituary was
published of a woman, Katrina Haslip, whom

the *New York Times* deemed prominent, worthy
of public memory. Katrina Haslip had died of
complications from AIDS. She was 33. She
was a former New York state prison inmate
who had been sent to prison after several
convictions for pickpocketing. While she
was in prison, she was diagnosed as HIV-
positive. Seeking help and finding none, she
founded an organization in prison to help
herself and the other ill inmates. After her
release, she continued her efforts to expand
awareness and resources for women with
AIDS. As the *Times* wrote," . . . Haslip joined
with other AIDS organizations . . . and

worked to press the federal government to expand its efforts to fight AIDS among women. . . . " Because of Haslip's work, said the *Times*, "the federal Centers for Disease Control and Prevention . . . a month before her death . . . announced plans to expand their definition of the disease to include more illnesses that affect women with AIDS. . . . " How many hundreds—thousands—of lives may have been eased, comforted, *saved* by the outpouring of funding and information that resulted?

Katrina Haslip. A pickpocket. Probably an addict. Possibly a hooker. In prison at the age of 27. Dead at 33. How could a losing hand like that be played to make the world a better place? And what is our excuse?

Just say yes.

I left my reading glasses in the refrigerator and
my driver's license in the back pocket of my
jeans through the rinse cycle. Three boxes of
huge Jiffy bags arrived when I needed tiny ones.
My complaint was answered with a fax of my
order: "huge" was written clearly in my
handwriting. When, to my relief, a substantial
check arrived, I paid some substantial bills.
What I neglected to do was deposit the check.
"You might be over-extended," a friend
suggested. "Nonsense," I replied, and rushed
off to Seattle wearing a jacket that, unnoticed

by me, was missing one dramatic shoulder pad.

This dementia was caused by my motto: Just say yes. Will you manage the community sit-down dinner for 100? Yes. Will you chair the awards committee? Yes. Will you bring doughnuts to the hospital on Friday? Yes. Will you come home this year and make sausage? Yes. Will you serve as secretary to the board? Yes. If I get a job, will you drive me? Yes.

It's a dangerous road to travel, and it reminded me of an article assignment I had to interview a white-collar heroin addict. This woman went through her Filofax one day and noticed that there wasn't a single name in it that didn't have something to do with buying, selling, or sharing drugs. This can happen in a just-say-yes world.

To the ancient Chinese curse "May you live in interesting times," we can add the feminist hex "May you live with unlimited options," and when they present themselves, just say yes. Losing your mind is a small price to pay for an interesting life.

And look for your car keys in the freezer.

Break hearts as you've been taught to
break eggs: with one sharp tap on the
side of the bowl.

We are quite willing, as age overtakes us, to abandon the fantasy of winning the swimsuit competition, but we are reluctant to forgo the title of Miss Congeniality. Instead of meeting the challenges of the workplace head-on—turn in the project on time and on budget, make a profit, meet sales goals, provide leadership to the staff—we worry about being nice, and we justify this by reciting our covenant that when we are in power, the world will be a kinder, gentler place. The fallacy is in the assumption that there is moral superiority in coddling someone's feelings so she will like us. This isn't ethics; this is egocentricity. The uncomfortable truth is that the right thing to do is sometimes the unpopular thing to do. That's why leaders—real leaders, not poll-sniffing politicians—have few friends.

People are both more resilient and less dependent than we give them credit for. The truth—presented openly, fairly, candidly with one sharp rap on the side of the bowl—bestows dignity. The message to the receiver is clear: You are an intelligent, resourceful adult who can recover from this pain and disappointment and move on. Godspeed.

If romances ended this way, *The Guiding Light* would have no plot lines. We say we can't bear to hurt him (translation: the awareness of his eternal devotion is a rush). Our ego basks in his assertions that he can't survive without us—right up to the day he calls and asks if his new friend ("You'll love her—she thinks Hackman's sexy, too!") can borrow your skis for a long weekend in Vail.

It's a rough life, but somebody's got to live it.

At a baby shower for a friend, I met the writer Mary Kay Blakely. She had recently published a book called *Wake Me When It's Over.* "What's it about?" I asked, and she replied, "It's the story of when I moved to Connecticut. I had little kids and no job, no money, no place to live. I ran around trying to make ends meet, and finally, I lapsed into unconsciousness and was in a coma for nine days." "A coma? What was the matter?" "Oh, nothing. Only burnout."

A coma. I had considered the ordinary solutions to stress: eat a pint of Ben & Jerry's ice cream, soak in the tub, shop 'til you drop, re-read all of Sue Grafton, watch a Katharine Hepburn marathon, henna my hair—but a coma really appealed to me: You're unreachable by phone and losing weight at the same time.

Take a tip from Mary Kay Blakely: If you choose a dramatic way to go on sabbatical, figure out a way to publish the experience.

Escape is a valid option.

The summer he was 12, your brother wrote a letter from camp that consisted of one sentence: "I'm doing ok but my roommates aren't too terrific but I guess I will ajust [*sic*]." When I was 12, I was sent to a co-ed church camp three hundred miles from home. Those were long miles. The journey took me from a tiny farm town to the suburbs of San Francisco, where, to my astonishment, girls who were "going into seventh" wore lipstick and bras. I didn't, which made me, in the vernacular of the '50s, a creep. When my cabinmates went to the pool, I, who did not fill out a bathing suit and therefore could not appear in public, lay on my bunk and wrote sad letters home. For part of one day I had a boyfriend, but at dinner he revealed that he was only "going into fifth." That humiliation struck the fatal blow to my dignity; my letters became tragic epistles. One afternoon a week later, the camp director came into the cabin and announced that my mother and my aunt had come to see me. They entered, shot me broad, knowing looks, and apologized profusely to the director for having to interrupt my jolly vacation but explained that there was a family emergency and I would have to leave. I forced a weak protest, stuffed my clothes into a footlocker, and escaped. That rescue was a subject of bitter contention in the family. My father was of the opinion that the real world was "like that" and that my mother and my aunt had been over-protective. I would never learn to stand on my own two feet, he predicted. "Those women" had taught me that I never had to suffer a difficult situation alone.

On that last point, he was right. In the intervening years, I cannot recall a time, even in the midst of failure and isolation, that I have felt truly alone. I have never lost faith that my prayers and my concerns, however trivial, are taken seriously and are answered. After all, decades ago when I was frightened and intimidated by girls with Tangerine lips and 32-AA charlies, I was saved. And if those imperfect mortals in my family have such generous spirits, what can I expect of One who is perfect?

Escape is not always the answer—but the question is: Is this a valuable lesson or an unnecessary torture?

When your brother's letter arrived, I packed my bags. And waited. Just in case he decided he couldn't "ajust."

As the classics teach us, hubris angers the gods.

In India, the Untouchables name their children Ugly Dirt and Scrawny Pig to fool the perverse immortals who, thinking the children are unloved, will let them live. Career success is equally vulnerable to the ravages of the spiteful. In America, when asked, "How's it going?" suppress the desire to respond, "Incredible! I may be taping a new album in London next week, and this outrageous guy I met at a black-tie dinner at the Waldorf—I told you I was up for a Pulitzer, didn't I?—is meeting me over there." A sly New Yorker tells this story: "As a kid, I lived across the street from Jack, an investment banker. Whenever I saw him, I'd say, 'Hey, Jack, how's business?' and he'd always say, 'Turrrrrible,' climb into his new Cadillac, and drive away."

Become a psalm reader.

If the passionate words of a nomadic Semite
who lived five thousand years ago speak to the
hearts of middle-aged Protestant women in
South Dakota who renew themselves in
Benedictine monasteries, perhaps it might be
worth our time to tune in. For starters, there's
no better way to, as the therapists say, work out
your anger. Having problems with people at
work? Try verses 1–8 of Psalm 35. I especially
relish "Fight those who are fighting me . . . let
them be overtaken by sudden ruin, caught in

their own net, and destroyed." Don't fritter the
day away plotting revenge; belt out one to the
Lord and be done with it.

Now, put away childish things.

A memory from a late afternoon in mid-June, 1966: I am sitting at my desk in the reception foyer looking out the window of a two-story Los Angeles office building that had once been a motel. The offices were layered around a fenced pool area clogged with bougainvillea and ficus trees. No one ever used the pool. Daydreaming, I had a sudden, stone-in-the-stomach realization that I would never use the pool, either—that, in fact, this summer I wouldn't be using anybody's pool: I wouldn't be having a summer vacation. True, I could take two weeks sometime after

September, when I would have worked a full year, but I wouldn't have the summer off. Not this year and not any year until kingdom come. The final curtain on my childhood fell.

You will be expected to release the totems of innocence: panda and Barbie and the top bunk; borrowing cars and crashing on sofas and charging on my account; tank-tops and Ding-Dongs and hitchhikes to Tierra del Fuego. The losses will be compensated by grown-up pleasures. But nothing will replace those endless, sepia summers when the lake lapped at our toes and each moment was crystalized by the fresh promise of fall.

Have courage.

A tough concept for a woman, courage: legends tell us that courage is pulling your buddies from a foxhole under heavy artillery fire or rushing through a burning building to save your children. We can do these things—but we'd rather find a definition that will work for us without the circumstances of Armageddon.

Before the novelist Jean Rhys died, she was interviewed for the *New York Times* by the writer Mary Cantwell. "Miss Rhys," Cantwell gushed, "you've led such a courageous life."

Rhys scoffed. "It wasn't courage," she said. "It was a stubborn determination to be happy."

From the crucible of experience and pain, the stubbornly determined—the courageous—can extract joy. Above all, I pray you grasp this strength.